Finding Grace

DAILY COMFORT FOR
UNCERTAIN TIMES

EIMAN AL ZAABI

BALBOA.PRESS
A DIVISION OF HAY HOUSE

Balboa Press books may be ordered through booksellers or by contacting:

Balboa Press
A Division of Hay House
1663 Liberty Drive
Bloomington, IN 47403
www.balboapress.com
844-682-1282

Because of the dynamic nature of the Internet, any web addresses or
links contained in this book may have changed since publication and
may no longer be valid. The views expressed in this work are solely those
of the author and do not necessarily reflect the views of the publisher,
and the publisher hereby disclaims any responsibility for them.

The author of this book does not dispense medical advice or prescribe the use
of any technique as a form of treatment for physical, emotional, or medical
problems without the advice of a physician, either directly or indirectly. The
intent of the author is only to offer information of a general nature to help
you in your quest for emotional and spiritual well-being. In the event you use
any of the information in this book for yourself, which is your constitutional
right, the author and the publisher assume no responsibility for your actions.

Print information available on the last page.

ISBN: 978-1-9822-3594-9 (sc)
ISBN: 978-1-9822-3596-3 (e)

Library of Congress Control Number: 2019915271

Balboa Press rev. date: 05/26/2021

Contents

Introduction

These are times of great uncertainty. Each day, we hear unsettling news from every corner of the world. Social and political polarization is increasing. Hateful speech fans the flames of violence. Long-held values like compassion and respect seem to be eroding. Materialism and greed have left whole segments of society economically insecure. Technology and social media have stolen the intimacy of our personal interactions, pressuring us to prioritize appearances over true connection. Environmental degradation continues, and we are now living with unprecedented, real effects of climate change, leaving us questioning whether we will be able to turn things around.

We humans have always found life to be uncertain, even under the best of circumstances. But today, we have moved from individual experiences of uncertainty in our daily lives to a shared unrest that brings a deep sense of anxiety crawling beneath our skin. Uncertainty scatters us like feathers in the wind. We are not sure where we are going and when the nightmare of our worst reality will end. We long for answers, seeking reassurance that we will be okay and that there is a secure future for our children.

The cumulative effect of this turbulence can be exhausting. We may have trouble sleeping or, worst of all, become apathetic. We begin to wonder: How long can this go on? How long can *I* go on? Responding to the challenges of the modern world is an endurance event, not a sprint. It's essential that we learn how to swim through the dark waves to reach the light.

Coping with today's reality begins with understanding that chaos is a force for growth. In any complex system, including the entirety of life on earth, every outcome is very sensitive to small differences in initial conditions. Chaotic systems naturally move between stability and instability, and this ebb and flow—whether expressed within a flock of birds migrating, a solar storm, or a human society—is a dynamic force that drives change. Evolution does not happen in stable systems or during tranquil times.

Because of the scale of the problems we are facing—climate change, widespread poverty, and political instability—it's tempting to assume that ordinary humans are just helpless victims. We might feel that we have no choice but to wait and see how things turn out. Yet each of us has a role to play, and we must take responsibility. Each of our actions has effects on other people and on this planet. These are among the tiny changes that instigate evolution. We bear responsibility for our footprint in the world. With every action we take, we choose either that which supports us or that which strains us, as individuals or as a collective.

The Divine is speaking to us through all of our current challenges. It's time we listened. The chaos of today's reality is part of a harmonizing effect in the universe, a push and pull meant to reveal a larger truth. When we understand that our choices have a larger impact, we can evolve beyond our everyday roles and move into conscious living. In this state of awareness, we can't help but do good in the world. We realize that at this critical time, our contribution matters. Chaos provides us with the opportunity to heal the world. It creates purposeful instability that pushes us to start anew. Chaos and uncertainty awaken the warrior within us who seeks truth and justice.

As human beings, we must acknowledge that we cannot control or even predict the future. All we can control are our intentions, our thoughts, the choices we make, and the actions we take. Beyond our limited sphere of influence lies the Divine. From our limited perspective, the world can seem random, heartless, and even cruel. Yet we can take comfort in the knowledge that unpredictability is in fact Divine order that we do not yet understand. Everything in this world is following the Divine's road map.

The antidote to uncertainty is not certainty; it is surrender to the Divine – the ultimate power who cares for and guides his creation. We may think that we suffer because we are uncertain of the future, when in truth it is because we are uncertain of our Creator's love. When faith dwindles in our hearts, we lose hope and spiral into a deep sense of despair. Expecting uncertainty and learning to anchor it through our connection with the Divine allows us to ride the turbulent waves of change and land safely on the shore. What a relief it is to say, "I accept. I surrender!"

Understanding that we are supported is transformative. It is grand to know that the sophisticated body that carries you has a Creator who lovingly and intelligently designed it as you were bestowed the gift of existence. Our souls lead our lives, and we travel in communion with our Creator. We take action based in truth and values, and we surrender the outcomes to the Divine. We acknowledge change, and we embrace it. We weave a spiritual nest in which we feel safe and can grow to our full potential. A life of growth is not about igniting the fire of change; it's about who you become once the ashes settle on the ground.

Human nature is like a closed flower bud. It can open only when we acknowledge its goodness and its desire to do good in the world. Deep within, we carry the knowledge of our purpose on this planet. Deep inside, we already know how these troubled times fit into the bigger picture of our individual and collective destiny.

The choice we have right now is to hang on to the thread that is the essence of our true humanity. If we let go of what makes us truly human – if we fail to reflect that in our ecological, economic, and social systems – we will lose our sense of who we really are and fall into total despair and helplessness. But if we accept the invitation to act from our true and moral self, we realize that we have the power – and, indeed, the responsibility – to change the world for the better. Beauty, joy, truth, peace, creativity, happiness, and respect are things we seek and value as humans. The well inside of us requests to be continuously filled. The human spirit seeks truth, and in that truth it finds its solace.

At this turning point, as the Divine witnesses our collective choice, there's room for our spiritual selves to lead us to a more just, humane, and harmonious existence. All change begins with a sincere prayer, an intention dedicated to the Creator of all there is, followed by restorative actions that can bring back the smile on the face of a troubled refugee or regrow the lungs of the planet. Life can flourish again on earth if we are able to save the human spirit from the beast of disconnection.

In this book, I offer you 365 inspirations, one for each day of the year. My hope is that they will provide you with the opportunity to reflect and to consciously build a new perspective that will enable you to live with grace in times of chaos and uncertainty. Think of the inspirations as seeds that will grow in the garden of your soul, giving you comfort and ease. Comfort is your home state; it is achieved by embracing the reality that surrounds you. A spiritual perspective grounded in truth will define the quality of your life experience and will allow you to masterfully sail toward a harmonious existence regardless of the storms that might hit your shore.

Change is inevitable, and its speed can be exhausting, but be assured that through that change you will form a new reality in which strength, resilience, and most importantly a state of surrender will carry you forward. You may see old dreams and desires collapsing in the midst of chaos, but as you allow the Divine to guide you with grace to the door of your true human self, surrender and acceptance will become your natural state, and you will float effortlessly towards your dreams. Your new perspective will lift you up and give you wings to fly. You will most certainly realize your true destiny as you make your contribution on planet Earth.

Becoming

Dare to scream until the birds fly
Dare to share your care with those who need it
Dare to walk away from the self you constructed
Discover a new land where the real you
Has invited you to a feast
Enter before the sun sets
And pray in thanks as you step
On the shores of paradise

Eiman Al Zaabi

PART 1

Winter

Winter is a quiet, peaceful season. The sun is low in the sky, and the light is soft. In cooler parts of the world, many plants lose their leaves and stop growing. The landscape appears inert and lifeless, but in truth every living thing is gathering its strength for the season to come.

Consider the tulip. Above ground, it appears that nothing is happening. Yet below the soil, the bulb is converting stored nutrients into new growth for the following spring. The wintertime dormancy is private and invisible, yet it is essential to the plant's future vitality.

We humans naturally follow similar seasonal cycles, although modern life makes it easy to lose touch with this fact. Winter is an ideal time to go inward and center yourself, just as nature does. This season, we'll explore themes of connection (and disconnection), simplicity, trust, and faith.

Connection

DAY 1

It is the soul's lifeblood to constantly be connected with the Divine. There is no separation between the present moment and the Divine presence. We live and breathe within that larger spiritual realm. Everything around you speaks the story of creation. Every animal, tree, or planet carries the truth of creation, and so do you.

DAY 2

Your soul knows exactly where it has come from, and it carries a lingering desire to connect to its Source.

DAY 3

True happiness starts with the spiritual dimension of life. Whatever changes you desire, strengthening your connection to the Divine will empower you to achieve them. Recognize that you can only begin where you are. Then set your intentions and allow the power of surrender to carry you forward. Let the loving guidance of the Divine be the rudder that steers you toward your best possible life.

DAY 4

When we feel we are at the mercy of life, without control or influence, we can become fearful or hopeless. When we reconnect with the Divine, we gain access to a deep well of strength and a profound source of guidance.

DAY 5

To achieve our spiritual goals, including a life of happiness and balance, we need to acknowledge where the disconnection lies in our lives. Where are we not being ourselves? Where are we not feeling connected to our surroundings? Where are we lost in our understanding of and connection to the Divine?

DAY 6

Even if we are driven by a feeling of purpose, no true meaning exists if we do not understand life on a spiritual level.

DAY 7

Aligning to the Divine power that has
masterfully created this universe is
the ultimate human pilgrimage.

DAY 8

Understanding the deep relationship
that ties us with the Divine helps us
realize that we move in communion, we
move in prayer, and we act in grace.

DAY 9

Pain is a sure sign of an imbalance. So are fear, anxiety, or depression. These things alert you that something requires your attention.

DAY 10

The purpose of life is to fully experience darkness and light, and to be privileged to choose one over the other.

DAY 11

Suffering is not exactly the same thing
as pain. Whether we are experiencing
physical, emotional, or mental pain,
it is the mental attitude toward our
circumstance that adds to the pain and
magnifies it to create suffering. Pain may
be our reality, but suffering need not be.

DAY 12

Whatever we hold at the level of thought,
emotion, and spirit translates directly
into experiences of either happiness and
peace or chaos and dissatisfaction.

DAY 13

We may approach life challenges as if they
are individual problems that we can solve
by ourselves if we just discover the right
strategy or remedy, make the right change,
or improve ourselves in some way. But these
are not separate issues defined by their
specifics; they are all the outcomes of a single
underlying process: disconnection from
the Divine and from our own true self.

DAY 14

Disconnection is the root cause of all
suffering. It starts when we disengage from
or dismiss the Divine presence, and it leads
us to essentially reject ourselves, our true
nature, and our purpose in this life.

DAY 15

Divisiveness and anger take us further
from the path that leads to the truth.

DAY 16

When we connect to the Divine, we embody
universal truths in our own particular way,
with the steadiness that comes from faith.

DAY 17

By listening carefully and cultivating
our connection to the Divine, we
receive both comfort and guidance.

DAY 18

Finding and knowing the Divine is what allows
grace to enter your life. Connection to the
Divine creates an enduring sense of flow. Even
when there are challenges in your life, the
conversation with the Divine need not cease.

DAY 19

Inner disconnection creates ripples into
our outer circumstances and environment,
leading to more pain and suffering for
ourselves and those around us.

DAY 20

Our task as humans is to align ourselves with
our true nature and the truth of the universe.
Disconnection from the Divine is at the root
of all the suffering we experience during our
lifetime. By learning to reconnect with and
surrender to the Divine, we give ourselves
the gift of true happiness and well-being.

DAY 21

How will our collective well-being change when
we recognize that when one of us is hurt, all
of us are hurt, and when we deliberately bring
harm to someone, we bring it to ourselves?

DAY 22

Struggle is not the problem; indeed, challenges
and even chaos can strengthen us, just as a tree
on a windy hillside develops a stronger trunk.
The real problem is in forgetting your roots
and distancing yourself from your true self.

DAY 23

When we dissociate from our true selves,
we cannot live to our fullest potential.

DAY 24

When you acknowledge that spirituality happens
in every moment, you make a leap of faith. Any
time you embody or act from love, any time
you live from a selfless place, you bring yourself
closer to the Divine. Any time you look at
someone with a compassionate heart and do your
best to honor that person, a piece of yourself is
restored, and you feel aligned and connected.

DAY 25

The wish to find, connect with, and surrender
to the Divine is like a flame burning inside
each one of us. It is the most powerful
intention we can set, and it clears the way for
us to fulfill the intention of our creation.

DAY 26

What if we all—across all religions, colors, and
backgrounds—acknowledge the oneness of
our Creator? How will our lives be different?
How will the planet look? How will such
alignment affect the way we interact with
each other? How will we as individuals behave
in the world? How will our communities
be transformed by the feeling of unity?

DAY 27

We can invite the awareness of the Divine
presence into the small and large aspects
of our lives. In the moments when we tie
the laces of our shoes, and in the moments
when we paint, write, and garden, we witness
the Divine's beauty and intelligence. In the
moments when we are angry, sad, or in
conflict, we see how these expressions can
allow Divine grace to enter our lives.

DAY 28

The Divine is present every minute of our
lives. The moment we realize his presence,
we remember our sacred connection.

DAY 29

Oneness and unity among all people is only
half the equation. Think of your relationship
with the Divine as a figure eight or infinity
symbol, with one side being you and the other
side being the Divine. Nothing in this world—
nothing—matters unless it takes us back to God.

DAY 30

It is the soul's essence, not your
limited human imagination, that
opens the door to true happiness.

DAY 31

As you seek to sustain connection to the Divine,
it is natural to have episodes of disconnection.
These are calls to establish a new and deeper
level of connection. A new truth wants to be
revealed in your experience, and the only way
you can uncover it is to move between the
states of connection and disconnection.

DAY 32

Life is a dance between connection and
disconnection, and every time we reestablish
our connection, we learn something new
about our spirituality that would not
have been possible for us to learn had
we not experienced disconnection.

DAY 33

Do you feel unsettled, as if there's
something missing in your life? Do you
feel on your own, without the support of
your Creator? That's how you know your
soul is longing for spiritual alignment.

DAY 34

Your destiny is a surrendered soul that flows
like a river in the garden of Divine connection.

Ways of Being

DAY 35

Be authentic. Align your words and
actions with your innermost values.
Listen to the voice within, and follow the
path of peace and harmony regardless
of what is happening around you.

DAY 36

The key to living a fully realized life is to
pay attention to values. These are ways to
be, not things to do. A goal is a destination;
we can arrive there and yet be unsatisfied,
feeling unsure where to go next. Values
are like directions on the compass; we
always know which way to travel.

DAY 37

Your values provide a vision for your best
possible life. Knowing your values is essential
to true happiness and well-being.

DAY 38

Each of your values contributes its own
complementary piece to a holistic picture
of the life the Divine intends for you.

DAY 39

Your values must be authentically yours.
They are as personal as your fingerprint.
As you consider your values, set aside any
notions about what other people value or
what you think you "should" value.

DAY 40

You can pinpoint one of your values by noticing
what gives you a feeling of "wrongness" and
then asking what would be the opposite. If
you are offended by callousness or disregard
for people who are vulnerable, perhaps
compassion is a central value for you.
Sometimes seeing what you don't want will
inform you of what you truly do want.

DAY 41

Let life change, but not your values.

DAY 42

You can always choose to do
things with integrity.

DAY 43

The secret to balance resides in the intersection
of what is natural and what is moral.

DAY 44

When you infuse your life with your values,
your choices are true to your soul. Every action
becomes an authentic reflection of who you
really are: a unique creation of the Divine.

DAY 45

The soul seeks situations and experiences in
which it is being its fullest self. It also seeks
to release old ways of looking at the world.

DAY 46

Ways of being, for the soul, include the experience of positive emotions and frequencies such as love, joy, freedom, compassion, truth, beauty, serenity, peace, and trust. Each soul comes with a unique signature blend of these states, which define its distinct essence, and so it thrives in this life as it seeks these states.

DAY 47

When the soul finds its own ways of being, it is reflecting the essential form given to it by the Divine.

DAY 48

Nourish yourself emotionally by looking for
experiences and environments that will provide
you with the ways of being that are unique to
you. If you value curiosity, engage in study and
research. If it's vital to you to be in the peaceful
state that comes from connecting with nature,
spend time outdoors. Satisfying these needs
can be easy and simple if you notice them
and give them space to grow in your life.

DAY 49

While we may not be able to see the destination
encoded in our dreams and desires, we do have
the ability to discern our intended states of
being. These can guide us, just as a compass
does. We may not know what to do, but we can
figure out how we would like to be, and that
insight can lead us in the right direction.

DAY 50

Have you secretly dreamed that one day you
will land in some sacred place where all of
your life's troubles disappear? The illusion
that our life can be fixed by abandoning it is
admittedly very tempting. But the reality you
live and breathe now is your spiritual path.

DAY 51

You will not find the answers any place
other than where you are. I invite you
to begin to look at your everyday life
differently, to allow it to have the light and
the sacredness it is supposed to have.

DAY 52

It is the reconnection with the Divine, not a disconnection from daily life, that transforms us.

Trust

DAY 53

When we have been so thoroughly steeped in a culture that convinces us of the power and value of sheer effort, we may see surrender as failure. In fact, surrendering is an act of great courage. It takes a lot of wisdom and faith to let things be.

DAY 54

While Divine wisdom supports our highest and best interest at all times, it sometimes doesn't appear that way because our knowledge and understanding of life is limited. Trust and let God move you forward with grace.

DAY 55

It can be hard to trust when the road ahead
is unknown. Relax into the knowledge
that there is an intelligent Divine power
that has your best interest at heart.

DAY 56

Trust is a form of surrender. When we trust,
we are creating the reality that is meant to be
by letting go of the things we can't control and
surrendering the outcomes to the Divine.

DAY 57

To let go and ask for guidance may challenge our desire for control, but it is only by surrendering to the Divine that we declare our humanness and recognize that the same gentle and loving power that feeds the birds in the sky and the fish in the deep sea has already taken care of our needs, too.

DAY 58

Sometimes the simplest moments are what we truly long for.

DAY 59

Trust the process of life regenerating itself; trust that you will be given what you have asked for.

DAY 60

Contentment is a subtler and more sustainable form of happiness. It comes from the realization that life is divinely guided. To change things for the better, we must surrender, understand the importance of timing, be willing to learn, and participate actively in life. To be content is to be satisfied with the way things are, to understand that where your life is at the moment is the right place for you.

DAY 61

Trust in the Creator who has imbedded
your purpose within you.

DAY 62

When the turtles lay their eggs on the
beach, they don't complain, *Why do I have
to do this every season and then leave my
eggs?* In nature, the qualities of trust and
surrender are always present. They are
essential to the life cycle of individuals
and to the larger, interconnected whole.

DAY 63

Most of us do not want to give up control.
We cling to the idea that we are fully able to
determine the outcomes in our lives. We set
expectations and we want them manifested. For
modern-day humans, it's a tough sell to believe
that there is a larger force at work. Yet the
Divine is always guiding you and caring for you.

DAY 64

When you surrender to the Divine, you
are surrendering to the power that has
nurtured you since you were an embryo in
your mother's womb, the power that has
masterfully operated and enlivened the
universe for more than thirteen billion years.

DAY 65

To trust the Divine is to say, "I am a creation of yours. You've given me the will to do things, but I need your light to find my way."

DAY 66

Life is dynamic and responsive in nature. While it isn't always clear to us why our lives are unfolding as they are, and certain moments may be very distressing, we can relax our need for control and trust in Divine guidance and wisdom instead.

DAY 67

It's a beautiful experience to witness how the Divine gives us what we ask for—or even better—when we pray from our hearts while trusting that our dreams will become reality.

DAY 68

The Divine is a lively and definite truth that shines throughout the universe.

DAY 69

Faith arises naturally in a heart that knows the Divine.

DAY 70

The Divine exists whether or not you believe.
Questioning and even doubt do not change
the truth of the Divine's existence. In fact,
they are what will lead you to the truth.

DAY 71

Finding the Divine is not about
proving; it is about awakening to
the truth that surrounds you.

DAY 72

At the depths of your soul, you will find
a place that is all-knowing and wise. That
place inside you is like your own sage or
elder. It has all the knowledge and wisdom
you need in order to find your path.

DAY 73

A faithful heart knows that it does
not need to feel despair.

DAY 74

Life is not about trying hard. It's about
learning how to sail smoothly.

DAY 75

When you despair, God will carry you.

DAY 76

Many of us get to know God at times of
crisis. We raise our flag and admit that
we cannot do life alone. We get in touch
with our humanness. We arrive at the
limit of what we can do or achieve on our
own. And there, we find the Divine.

DAY 77

The Divine has supreme control over
the workings of the universe.

DAY 78

There's always an ultimate power that holds
and governs the universe. When we accept
this, we access a place of profound security.

DAY 79

Finding the Divine is like finding water in
a desert. Your life is restored to its fullest.
You drink in the nectar of life, only to find
that all you need is already given to you.

DAY 80

Faith is felt on the level of the heart,
not the mind. It is not a mental concept
or idea, but rather a turning of the
heart that feels peaceful and true.

DAY 81

Your destiny lies in the hands of a loving God.

DAY 82

Life takes us on a journey, and there is always
the risk that it will be cut short. We know that,
and we learn to live with it as we carry our hopes
and desires between the bones of our rib cage.

DAY 83

In the grand scheme of things, each of us is a
single impression of light in the fabric of the
universe – a fabric that is billions of years old.

DAY 84

All is well. There is nothing you
need that is not given to you.

DAY 85

Can you set the intention to create an
opening for your true self to speak to you?

DAY 86

There is a creative side of us that wants to
initiate and push things forward. We must
balance that aspect of ourselves with the
willingness to be in patience, prayer, and
anticipation of what the Divine brings
into our life. It's a delicate equilibrium,
but with practice, it is entirely possible.

DAY 87

Surrender is a dance between an taking action and waiting. These are two sides of the same coin. Sometimes you'll decide to do what is necessary in a certain situation, and then you'll surrender the outcomes while waiting for the next thing to be revealed to you. At other times you will surrender a situation right from the beginning because you have no clue what to do. Be willing to flow between acting and waiting. Allow things to emerge organically.

DAY 88

Our dreams come to fruition at the
right time, when we are ready.

DAY 89

It's natural to feel impatient, but remember
that the timing of the answers you seek is
always up to the Divine. They come to you
when the soul is ready for change, for insight,
and for growth. Along your journey, you will
be accessing parts of the truth as your soul
is ready to take the insight and turn it into
action. Do not be frustrated or disappointed
if you don't get your answers right away.

DAY 90

There is no need to judge your life as it is now, or
to be overwhelmed by the change that needs to
take place. Everything happens at the right time.

DAY 91

The present moment is where our happiness lies, whether the present is a moment of struggle or moment of pure joy. A life lived in these moments is a life that is lived fully.

PART 2

Spring

Spring is a time of renewal and change. Seedlings sprout, trees grow new leaves, and flowers burst forth. No matter how long the winter has been, springtime reminds us that new beginnings are always possible. But springtime is not just about sunshine and bright flowers. The weather is changeable, with gusty winds and heavy rain. While its restlessness may seem positive and hopeful, filled with life, it can also challenge us. A late frost can kill tender seedlings.

Spring reminds us that the purpose of chaos is to instigate evolution. With this in mind, we can welcome turbulence. Our experiences provide opportunities for us to evolve to our fullest potential, and our personal evolution is intimately connected with the evolution of the planet.

Self-Nourishment

DAY 92

To express your divine purpose by making
your intended contributions to the world,
you must nourish your spiritual self.

DAY 93

It is by meeting the needs of your
own soul that you prepare yourself to
nurture the world around you.

DAY 94

To find true well-being, we must begin by
attending to the needs of the soul. The
first and most important of these needs
is to find and connect to the Divine.

DAY 95

To meet the needs of your soul, start by creating practices to nurture yourself on the physical, emotional, mental, social, and spiritual levels.

DAY 96

Your body requires your attention and nourishment. It is the vehicle that carries you, the space in which the spirit moves and flows. It seeks to be used in adding to life and creating good in the world.

DAY 97

By focusing on our relationships with friends
and family, we gain a sense of support during
tough times. We discover opportunities to
exchange love with others as we express
our unique ways of being in the world.

DAY 98

Self-care matters just as much as caring for
others. To make a positive impact on the
world, we must first nourish ourselves.

DAY 99

We take the first step in meeting the soul's needs by creating practices to nurture ourselves on the physical level. Your soul can shine fully only through a body that is nourished by authentic foods and beverages, sunshine, and time outdoors.

DAY 100

When the world is in such great need of healing, we can overextend ourselves and become exhausted. Take it easy, care for yourself, and refresh your spirit.

DAY 101

Give yourself the gift of distraction-free time.
You will emerge clearer and more balanced.

DAY 102

Your wakeful consciousness is your
greatest strength and gift. Do not
compromise it with thoughtless distraction.
Own it, direct it, and use it!

DAY 103

Information overload kills creativity. Unplug
and make space for ideas to emerge.

DAY 104

When the world needs so much from us,
it may not feel right to focus on caring for
ourselves. But it is from a place of balance,
well-being, and even happiness that we
make our deepest contributions to the world.
Open your heart and let your soul shine
as you do the best you can in your family,
your community, and the outside world.

DAY 105

Self-nourishment gives you the
resilience and strength to weather tough
times and fulfill your purpose.

DAY 106

Self-nourishment is not selfish; it is
the foundation of a well-lived life.

DAY 107

Your emotions are a signpost for the growth
that needs to happen in your life.

DAY 108

We may believe we've been taking care of ourselves, when in fact we have been neglecting ourselves. The outside world distracts us with all of its conflict and chaos. It beckons us with false self-soothing. To be truly well, we must recognize the desires of the self that lies within. We must nourish ourselves spiritually.

DAY 109

Even if we sincerely intend to care for ourselves, a form of self-neglect can take hold when we do not pay attention to what's bubbling up inside of us. Nothing will truly nourish us unless we are tending to the inner self. Losing touch with your soul is like dying with your eyes open.

Growth

DAY 110

Is it self-indulgent to care for ourselves when there is so much misery and desperation in the world? Shouldn't we be directing our attention toward others? Quite simply, caring for others begins with caring for ourselves.

DAY 111

Pay attention to the inner self that wants something grander and more harmonious.

DAY 112

The nature of life is to grow us, to develop us toward fulfilling the purpose imprinted in us by the Divine, just as the warming soil tells the crocus bulb to unfurl.

DAY 113

In realizing the limits of our influence, we learn how to live from a place of wanting to grow and understand rather than wanting to control and manipulate. Life becomes our greatest experiment and our greatest opportunity for spiritual learning. We accept our humanness and embrace the role Divine power has in us realizing our fullest potential.

DAY 114

To be human is to be greedy, hasty, and loving at the same time. To be human is to embody all of these states, and to smooth the rough edges and allow the true self to come forth.

DAY 115

It takes real courage to listen to the distant call of your spiritual self. It takes even greater courage to shift the direction of your life.

DAY 116

True evolution happens when we shine the light on our shadow self and allow it to share with us the gifts and lessons it has in store.

DAY 117

In your darkest night, seek the light of faith.

DAY 118

In the face of harsh and unpredictable events,
when the world is nearly unrecognizable, it
may seem unsafe to express your creativity.
It's easy to feel that your future is no longer
in your hands. Yet as long as you are still
dreaming, you are capable of creating a channel
by which you can achieve those dreams.

DAY 119

Experiences in our lives reveal so many truths,
if we are observant enough to receive them.

DAY 120

When you breathe, life breathes back.

DAY 121

We will not find the answers in a bottle floating
in the sea. Only through our experience
do we know what we need to know.

DAY 122

When we feel a springtime urge to grow and renew ourselves, it may be because we have neglected one of our true needs. What is the state of your body? How is your emotional well-being? What is your typical mental state? How are your relationships? Do you have an active spiritual practice? Take an honest look at which parts of your life might need attention.

DAY 123

Sometimes unpleasant experiences emerge in order to teach us something new that will become a stepping-stone toward that which we desire.

DAY 124

When you feel crippling worry about
the future, remember that nothing in
this universe moves without divine
permission. Release your worries to God.

DAY 125

Life is evolutionary in nature. What's unwanted
is actually essential to equip the self with
the skills needed to fulfill its purpose.

DAY 126

Notice the little lessons that add to your
awareness and understanding of life.

DAY 127

Change may be motivated by pain or by hope.
In life, we tend to dance between both states.
Sometimes we change in response to a pain that
is present in our reality, and at other times we
grow toward a certain vision we'd like to achieve.

DAY 128

It's often the imbalances in our lives
that point us toward our path.

DAY 129

Life is always providing us with
whatever we need in order to grow.

DAY 130

To progress in life, hold an open heart and a
learning mind. Be willing to step back and
reflect on the message behind each situation.

DAY 131

Life is designed to keep us engaged.
Variety and change make us more likely
to find our way to the Divine, as we keep
learning and growing every day.

DAY 132

The same Divine power that created us
has placed us in a dynamic environment
that feeds us information when we need
it. Nothing we need in order to fulfill our
purpose as humans on earth is left out. We
have all the resources we need to form our own
comprehensive understanding of the universe.

DAY 133

Chaos theory tells us that in a dynamic system,
minor differences in initial conditions can create
unpredictable, far-reaching long-term results.
Our actions take place within a web that is
just as complex as the Earth's atmosphere.

DAY 134

Hold the intention to be a force of good in the world. When you show kindness and compassion, the forces of chaos will carry the ripples beyond the immediate situation and into the community and the larger world.

DAY 135

Chaos is powerful, but it is not random. Although we may find chaos uncomfortable, it is a productive and dynamic force driving growth. It is intended for the greater purpose of instigating evolution, both on a personal level and on a planetary level.

DAY 136

The universe is chaotic and unpredictable by nature. When all is well, we experience this truth as a source of great mystery, surprise, and delight. When events take an unsettling turn, the fundamental unpredictability of the world can make us feel anxious or even despairing. Either way, the nature of life is to grow us.

DAY 137

In life, each one of us is exposed to different inputs that shape us. Whether we experience them as positive or negative, they provide opportunities for us to evolve to our fullest potential. They are part of the Divine's plan for us.

DAY 138

Each one of us plays a role in other people's lives. We generate input for the psyches of those around us. Meanwhile, others are generating input for our own psyches. We shape each other's evolution as we grow to fulfill our potential.

DAY 139

While change and uncertainty may make us uneasy, they come with a beautiful and important gift. Chaos offers us a precious opportunity to meet one of the soul's deepest needs: to find ways to express its unique essence and qualities.

DAY 140

The unpredictability of world events may be uncomfortable, but it also allows us to view life differently. The universe is a divinely guided system in which growth is continually driven by the engine of chaos. Your personal evolution is tied to the evolution of the planet.

DAY 141

Day and night, male and female, truth and
falsehood, right and wrong—polarities
surround us wherever we go. Polarity is
a dynamic and productive force driving
growth and change. Polarities on the level
of human living encourage compassion and
collaboration. On the level of values, they
encourage the search for truth. At the level
of natural systems, they instigate change
and evolution. No matter the level at which
these polarities operate, they exist to create a
certain richness and force for positive change.

DAY 142

Everything around us is working in precision to create a harmonious ecosystem. The restfulness of night follows the activity of day in an unceasing, synchronous dance. It is easy for us to take these rhythms for granted, yet they are essential to our lives. The Divine is the orchestrator of harmony and has ensured this beautiful order through the interaction of the different polarities on all levels. Harmony is the truth from which the universe operates.

DAY 143

Polarities sometimes reveal themselves to us
in ways that are painful. For example, you
come to know the true meaning of health
and vitality after being sick for a while. The
issue here is not the existence of polarities
but the way the human mind labels them.
We think that one is positive and the other
is negative and undesirable. In reality,
the two are not opposites at all. They are
complementary. In experiencing them both,
we develop a deeper understanding of life.

DAY 144

Evolution happens as a result of life experiences.
Your experiences of responding to change and
challenge give you resilience and strength.

DAY 145

Evolution is the gift of life. Without it we would
not be able to realize our purpose. We would not
discover the answers to our biggest questions.
We would not love more or forgive more. We
would not move toward being fully human.

DAY 146

When we accept the truth that life is uncertain,
dynamic, and responsive, we understand
that life is our spiritual nest. Within it
we grow, we learn, we seek guidance and
support, and we fly as we use challenge as an
opportunity to realize our fullest potential.

Intention

DAY 147

Intention plays a vital role in moving
your life in the direction you choose. An
intention is an energy that involves a
wish for the future, plus a desire to act or
change accordingly in the here and now.

DAY 148

When we set a clear and honest intention to
do something, life seems to unfold more easily
and smoothly. We simply go with the flow as
we pursue what we would like to achieve.

DAY 149

Using intention skillfully is a two-step process.
First, acknowledge where you are. Then,
know where you are headed. Your intentions
define your results, so believe and intend!

DAY 150

Stop seeking success. Instead, seek to be fulfilled.

DAY 151

When you set an intention, you allow
for the emergence of the experiences
that will show you your path.

DAY 152

Allow your intention to be magnified by
the energy of pain or gain. Perhaps you are
determined to change your reality because you
are in pain. Or perhaps have a desire that you
very much want to bring to fruition. In either
case, the energy of your desire will strengthen
your intention and provide a context for
the change that is happening in your life.

DAY 153

Choose a theme – such as clarity – for the
day, month, or year. Then, as the year unfolds,
notice how you encounter opportunities
and lessons in line with that theme.

DAY 154

Sometimes we believe we have set an
intention, yet we subconsciously resist it.
Our actions are driven not by intention but
by whatever emotions we are feeling in the
moment. This clouding of our intention
undermines us and hinders the outcome.

DAY 155

If things are not working out as you wish,
ask yourself, "What am I gaining by not
having the outcome I seek?" Sometimes
we need to purify our intentions before
they will move us in the right direction.

DAY 156

When we align to the Divine, everything
is between us and God. This keeps us in
touch with the truth and maintains our
intentions on the highest level. We act
selflessly and give from the heart.

DAY 157

When you have a purpose and an intention,
the Divine will carry you as you move forward
with those actions. You will become a conduit
for positive change on earth, big or small.

DAY 158

Difficulty is an opportunity for growth and
evolution. It helps us develop the experience
and skills necessary to live a life of purpose
and meaning. Every challenge has the potential
to bring us closer to our life's purpose.

DAY 159

Along the path, there will be setbacks.
When things don't go as you'd hoped,
cultivate resilience by looking for the
lesson in the experience. There is wisdom
in every situation that you encounter.

DAY 160

Do not allow the motions of change to
take away the sweetness of your life.

DAY 161

You must know the darkness to know the light.

DAY 162

It is human nature to change states of
being and consciousness all the time.
Through all the changes, we anchor
ourselves in surrender and prayer.

DAY 163

Divine guidance is always available to you.

DAY 164

God will meet you wherever
and however you are.

DAY 165

Pleasure and pain are the two forces
for change. Embrace them, and you will
grow into the life of your dreams.

DAY 166

Pain is an inevitable part of the growth
process. It helps us realize that there's
something clouding our happiness. It draws our
attention so we can make needed changes.

DAY 167

Creativity requires a certain amount
of challenge to flourish.

DAY 168

Each of us, no matter what our path, faces
challenges in life. It's easy to feel alone
in our difficulties, but in truth they are
universal to the human experience.

DAY 169

In the eyes of the Divine, you are much more
than right or wrong. You will be looked at by
the infinite and Divine self that understands
why you did what you did. With the Divine,
these are facts more than judgments; they
simply describe your state of alignment or
misalignment to the universal truths.

DAY 170

Are you trying and trying to make things
happen, but with no luck? Do you feel that
if you let the situation go, the changes you
hope for will surely never arrive? It's easy
to feel that as long as we work hard and
keep trying, things will work themselves
out. But we operate in a universe governed
by the Divine, not by human will.

DAY 171

It is through prayer and surrender,
not effort, that we achieve our desires
and fulfill our highest purpose.

DAY 172

Challenges such as loss, anxiety, or dissatisfaction can be an opportunity to create a new reality, but only if we understand them fully.

DAY 173

The clamor of daily life can make it difficult to hear the voice of the soul. Our habits and everyday routines can blind us to new possibilities. There is tremendous value in taking a thoughtful break to reconnect with the soul and investigate what really matters to us. This kind of pause can reinvigorate us. It may even dissipate some of our struggles.

DAY 174

When a negative emotion or perspective
weighs you down, place a balancing
truth on the other side of the scale.

DAY 175

We create emotional resilience as we strengthen
our self-awareness and grow stronger from the
inside, developing greater compassion toward
ourselves and others and treating challenges
as opportunities to create a different reality.

DAY 176

You may sometimes wonder, Why am I always
challenged or troubled? Why aren't things
working for me? Such questions assume that
everything must be perfect all at once. The truth
is that life is revealed to us one day at a time.

DAY 177

Change is not always easy. Growth can
have a chaotic feel, just as a windstorm
can bring down tree branches. It's helpful
to remember that chaos is meant to evolve
us so we can fulfill our Divine purpose.

DAY 178

For every difficult situation, there's always
a question to move you forward.

DAY 179

Understand that change may happen gradually,
or it may show up sooner than anticipated.
It may also come in ways that you may not
understand or recognize at first, until you realize
that they are what you have been asking for.

DAY 180

Springtime reminds us that new
beginnings are always possible.

DAY 181

True alignment to the Divine takes place not in some other realm, but here and now, in our everyday life. It happens at the times when we are busy, distracted, and not focused. It happens at times of crisis. It happens when we are out with friends, discussing matters of life.

DAY 182

We can connect with and align to the Divine in every action we take.

PART 3

Summer

In the long days of summer, we naturally feel more energetic and expansive. This season is about stoking the fire inside of us to pursue healing for ourselves, our communities, and our planet. The soul yearns to bring healing by taking intentional, restorative actions. The goodness inherent in each of us is a river waiting to flow through.

But the wish to make things happen can sometimes lead to frustration or disappointment. When our efforts don't bring the results we wished for, we are confronted with questions about how much control we really have.

To bring our dreams to fruition, we must learn how to nurture our hopes while releasing the outcomes. There's a delicate balance between taking action (doing) and letting go (being). This is what will allow you to bring your dreams to reality and make your mark in this world.

So, in this season, we'll explore themes of control, free will, truth, dreams, and action. Your soul longs for a real and lasting connection with her destiny. Will you put aside your ego and let her take the lead?

Control & Free Will

DAY 183

Humans are created with the intention,
the blueprint, and the potential to find
the truth for ourselves. We are honored
with the gift of choice, and that is a great
distinction given to us by the Divine.

DAY 184

Our God-given free will presents us with
great challenges. It gives us the illusion of
power and control, when in fact we are not in
charge. While the rest of creation is already
in alignment with this universal truth, we
humans continually struggle to grasp it.

DAY 185

Our lives consist of a series of moments
outside of our control. Yet we also have
considerable influence and responsibility.
We are continually confronted with choices,
and what we choose at any given moment
determines the results we get while affecting
our overall happiness and well-being.

DAY 186

Some aspects of our lives appear to be within
our power to influence. The fact that we do
have a zone of influence—a gray area in which
we practice willpower—creates the illusion
that we are in control. Such illusion blinds us
to the presence of the Divine in our lives.

DAY 187

Having free will means that you have the
ability to make choices in a governed universe
with the resources you have in any given
moment. You do not control the outcomes;
they are not yours. You can certainly make
an impact with a particular action, but you
cannot guarantee the results. No human can.

DAY 188

To come to a crossroads and choose your own
path is the greatest privilege of being human.

DAY 189

In our limited capacity to control the outcomes of our lives, we forget that the planets, stars, trees, animals, and entire universe are in a state of surrender. The natural state of surrender is about knowing when to "do"—that is, when to exert our influence—and when to simply "be."

DAY 190

The responsibility of free will starts with setting positive intentions.

DAY 191

Surrender starts with acknowledgment of
our humanness and the Divine presence in
our lives, and it moves us toward the art of
applying our willpower in a spiritually aligned
universe to create good in the world.

DAY 192

Free will is not something we exert in a
random and arbitrary context. Rather, we are
on a journey in which the Divine guides and
supports us every step of the way. The beauty
and essence of the human connection with
the Divine lies in the delicate intersection
between willpower and Divine power.

DAY 193

Finding and connecting to the Divine frees us from struggle and fear by teaching us to surrender that which is outside our control.

DAY 194

Accept the privilege of choosing your path.

DAY 195

If we are not in control, why do we think we are? The illusion comes from being given the resources to make an impact. We manipulate the things at our fingertips, and when we see the outputs we expect, we develop the idea that we were fully responsible. Anything that we bring awareness to enters the circle of our apparent control. But the illusion of control is just that: an illusion.

DAY 196

When we decide to embrace surrender in our lives, we are asked to become more and more discerning of what is within our control and what is not.

DAY 197

Surrendering does not mean giving
up; it means understanding what we
can control and what we cannot.

DAY 198

True power comes not from control but from
your sacred relationship with the Divine.

DAY 199

If we dismiss the spiritual dimension of
our lives, we strip everything we witness
of its sacredness. We run in circles trying
to fix, control, and manipulate our life and
the lives of others. This is a fundamentally
imbalanced state. Understanding our
true nature brings us into balance.

DAY 200

In everything we set out to do, there's an
element of unpredictability alerting us
to the existence of a higher power that
is in charge. Yes, we are responsible for
our intentions and actions; however, the
outcomes are not always guaranteed.

DAY 201

Give up control and invite the
Divine to sail your boat.

DAY 202

The Divine self is where all power lies.

Truth

DAY 203

Life is based in truth. When we
follow a path that diverges from the
truth, life will bring us back.

DAY 204

Each of us is a student of life on this very
special planet, in this marvelously created
universe. We are all here to experiment and
learn. Our progress is based on our own
motivation to live authentically and truthfully
in alignment with the rest of creation. This is
our journey, but we must consciously claim it.

DAY 205

Make a decision that you know deep
within is based in truth, based in
love, and based in courage.

DAY 206

When you see beauty, you perceive the truth.

DAY 207

Make a home for your soul in your
daily consciousness by speaking truth,
seeking truth, and being in truth.

DAY 208

Inquiry connects you to truth and
ultimately to the Divine.

DAY 209

Joy is the felt experience of being in truth.

DAY 210

Let your heart be tender enough to
hear the whispers of truth.

DAY 211

Shed whatever is not truthful.

DAY 212

Truth always attracts resistance.

DAY 213

As we travel our path, we uncover glimpses of the infinite qualities of the Divine. These qualities teach us how to trust and surrender. Wherever we turn—night or day—the Divine is revealing his beauty through his creation.

DAY 214

Each truth that is revealed to you is part of
a larger, unified, holistic truth that you are
continuously uncovering as you move along.

DAY 215

The truth we are seeking is right before
our eyes. It shows us the way into an
eternal life that we are waiting to enter.

DAY 216

Truth is a safe land to be in. It
feels like home to the soul.

DAY 217

Acknowledging the truth of God puts you in tune with the rest of creation. Your life comes to resonate with the universal truths, and you begin to find your nest of balance and harmony.

DAY 218

When you commit to finding the truth and living with integrity, your soul begins to direct your life. Your presence has the quality of being connected and grounded at the same time. You exude confidence as you know that all is well.

DAY 219

Do not shy from speaking truth
in the face of darkness.

DAY 220

Our well-being is intimately tied to our inquiry
into ourselves and our surroundings. In the
space of exploration, we learn the meaning of
our existence as a species, we learn what feeds
our soul, and we learn the true meaning of
happiness in the midst of change and chaos.

DAY 221

The fact that we exist to experience the Divine is reason enough to exist at all.

DAY 222

The human heart is equipped with the intelligence to find and recognize the truth.

DAY 223

We are by nature spiritual beings who long to connect with our world and the other people within it. Everything around us has the potential to inspire questions that will lead us to the truth.

DAY 224

It's disorienting to realize that we live in a world of illusion and deception. In every realm of life, from politics to spirituality, someone is ready to manipulate us or sell us something. What can we trust? Where does the truth lie? Now more than ever, it is essential to align ourselves with the Divine, identify our values, and express our unique purpose in the world.

DAY 225

As you move deeper into the mystery,
issues and problems play a smaller role
in your life. It becomes your mission
to feed your soul with truth.

DAY 226

Integrity means the quality of being in
resonance or alignment with the universal
truths. To bend integrity is to break a
spiritual promise that resides within us. That
internal break stays with us. It manifests
in our life in different forms, including
disconnection from our true self and the
Divine. In a sense, we have betrayed ourselves
by dismissing a truth known in our heart.

DAY 227

Death is a fact of life. It is our teacher, prompting us to learn to live fully, to wake up to the truth around us.

DAY 228

In times of crisis, attune to the call of your soul and answer it. Follow your heart, act on your values, and connect to your Creator for guidance and solace.

DAY 229

Nature is the river from which we drink Divine truth. It is there that we ask questions and receive our answers.

DAY 230

The truth is not difficult to find; we are
simply invited to wake up to it.

DAY 231

Joy and expansion come to you when
you align to the truth of creation.

DAY 232

Our souls rejoice as we expand the learned
truth into our entire being, dancing in
resonance with the rest of creation.

Dreams

DAY 233

Dreams are all about expression of the soul. They are the outlet through which we become our best selves and contribute our goodness to the world.

DAY 234

When we can see clearly what we want to achieve, we have the power to bring something into being and then nurture it.

DAY 235

Don't worry if your dreams seem overwhelming.
It's not your job to bring every one of
these desires to fruition. Rather, your
responsibility is to acknowledge them, listen
to their messages, and let them inspire your
spirit. The role of the Divine is to give you
opportunities to express your dreams, to
build a life of meaning and contentment.

DAY 236

Become the container that will tenderly hold
the beauty of your dreams. Feed them ideas.
Nourish them with your willingness. Then
take actions that will give them form.

DAY 237

Hope is a whisper of the aspiring heart.

DAY 238

There are many paths toward realizing our dreams. When we visualize just one and then focus on that, we may pursue a dead end and fail to recognize any of the paths that would actually take us there.

DAY 239

Our dreams and desires are not fixed mental
images that seek to be realized. Rather, they
serve as indicators. They point us toward
the states of being we'd like to achieve
by pursuing a certain dream or goal.

DAY 240

During crisis, dreams are no longer wishes
but moral obligations we must pursue.

DAY 241

The door to heaven lies in your heart.

Action

DAY 242

Your relationship with the Divine is not only about receiving but also about giving. Through your actions, you make your unique and precious contributions to the world as you express the purpose of your creation.

DAY 243

We are drawn to serve and contribute by expressing the soul's unique gifts. This is prayer in action.

DAY 244

Actions are the bridge between the inner
world and the outer world. When you live in
integrity, your understanding of the Divine will
most certainly be reflected in what you do.

DAY 245

The Divine wants you to express the
extraordinary side of yourself – the creative,
informal, free-flowing side of yourself,
the side that is filled with love and joy and
wants to make a mark in the world.

DAY 246

What area of need calls to you? Let go of
thoughts about what you "should" care
about, and instead ask yourself what
you feel genuinely passionate about.

DAY 247

Every one of us is meant to add to the
world in a way that no one else can. If you
do not act, that contribution is lost.

DAY 248

Let this be your time to wake up and create
a magnificent ripple that touches your
life and every other life on the planet.

DAY 249

Every human's life counts. Every contemplation,
every word of truth you say, and every
action in service of others counts.

DAY 250

In times of upheaval, harness your fear and
anger and use them to discover your role in
creating the future. Rather than succumbing
to helplessness, unleash your personal
power to make the change you have always
dreamed of. Clarify your role, and seek
positive, peaceful ways to make an impact.

DAY 251

With the support and guidance of the Divine,
you can confidently speak your truth. You
can set positive intentions and then take
the steps to bring your vision into reality.

DAY 252

Let your actions be guided both by knowledge
and by knowing. Knowledge is based on
history, study, and past experiences. Knowing,
on the other hand, is intuitive. You will need
both in order to take informed action.

DAY 253

Each one of us is like a single drop in a big
sea. Alone we are quite small, but together we
are mighty. Each drop transmits the energy
to create powerful waves and currents.

DAY 254

When harsh words bring forward the worst
in human nature, fanning flames of hatred,
it is essential that each of us – all around the
globe – rise to the occasion. The challenge we
face is opportunity in disguise. In this unsettling
time, we must take ownership of our lives
and our communities. It's a chance to identify
what we care deeply about, and take action.

DAY 255

The soul longs to find ways of expressing its beauty. It is here that we embody our talents, our abilities, and our most hidden desires for ourselves and the world.

DAY 256

Your contribution matters.

DAY 257

Take responsibility for your actions and your impact.

DAY 258

Do not allow feelings of sadness, hopelessness, outrage, or fear to paralyze you. Let them instead motivate you to purposeful action.

DAY 259

Every time you have an insight or make a decision, include the awareness of your soul's need for truth. Ask yourself, Does this support my well-being? Is it in alignment with what I know to be true of the Divine?

DAY 260

A soul aligned with the Divine is by nature a compassionate soul that desires to act with love and kindness.

DAY 261

When you are in a state of giving, acting in
prayer, you live your life from the inside out.
You heed your soul's eager call to connect with
the Divine and then express its gifts. You share
your uniqueness, your brilliance, and your light.

DAY 262

Don't be discouraged by the magnitude of the
problems or the amount of work to be done.
It's not possible to save the world all at once –
or all alone. Take one small step at a time.

DAY 263

Every action, large or small, can be an
expression of what matters to us.

DAY 264

Your sincere actions – even the smallest
ones – may go much further than you
realize. Every one of us has the power
to make a difference on this planet.

DAY 265

We must respond to the dark aspects of
humanity by being the light. We know that we
will not achieve perfection in creating a better
world, but as long as we shall live, we can pledge
to cast the bright glow of love and the cool
waters of peace wherever they are needed.

DAY 266

If you allow hopelessness to paralyze
you, you will deprive the world of the
contribution only you could make.

DAY 267

A life that expresses your gifts, your
faith, and your Divine purpose is a life
fully owned and worth living. Have no
doubt that it will change the world.

DAY 268

Every action ripples outward. You can
change the world from within your
circle of influence, wherever you are
and however you are called to help.

DAY 269

As we seek ways to express our purpose, we
must understand that we cannot predict
or control the outcomes. All we can control
are our intentions, the choices we make,
and the actions we take. Beyond our limited
sphere of influence lies the Divine.

DAY 270

Instead of asking "How can I save the world,"
ask "What are the unique things I have to
offer? How can I be a force of good right here,
right now?" When you approach life this way,
"saving the world" is no longer something you
might manage to accomplish in the future
if only you could figure out how. It becomes
something you do all the time, with every
action you take, in every aspect of your life.

DAY 271

No choice is too small to make a difference.

DAY 272

It's possible that you will never know
the full impact of your actions.

DAY 273

Once you've taken action, let it be,
having faith that Divine guidance
will illuminate your next steps.

DAY 274

The awakening of a single human being has
the potential to create a significant ripple
effect on that person's family, friends,
community, and planet. A drop of water
joins other drops to create an ocean. In
there lies your power as an individual.

PART 4

Fall

Fall is a time of harvest. We see how the seeds planted in the spring have come to fruition. We see how our efforts have moved us closer to our goals, or perhaps further away. This is a time to appreciate the power of the human mind, where intentions and plans are born – and also where unproductive worry may arise. It's a time to consider how we are fulfilling our purpose in life. It's a time to reflect on our relationship with the Divine, to notice the limits of our influence and commit ourselves to our role in the partnership of prayer and surrender.

At this point in the seasonal cycle, we are reminded of the bounty and generosity that surrounds us and, at the same time, of our own limits and vulnerabilities as humans. We can take comfort in knowing that we are guided and protected in every step of our journey, and that the path ends in a return home to our Creator.

Mind

DAY 275

Your time, focus, and energy are your
most precious resources. It's essential to
be selective about how you use them.

DAY 276

Reclaim your life by turning away from
distractions and committing yourself to your
higher purpose. Embrace the present moment
and rejoin the reality that surrounds you.

DAY 277

It's when the spiritual and the
mundane merge together that we align
with the meaning of our life.

DAY 278

Beyond the rumbling of emotions, there
lies a self that is serene and pristine.

DAY 279

We face an endless onslaught of distractions.
Social media, text messages, and news feeds
continually demand our attention, bombarding
the mind with stimulation until it is numb
to its instinctive search for purpose and for
the Divine. We become passive participants,
forgetting that we were brought here for a
reason that requires our active participation.

DAY 280

Your life is a precious gift that should not
be squandered in mindless distraction.

DAY 281

What are the measures by which you
know you are living a good life?

DAY 282

Let the unpredictability of the world fire your
curiosity. Let the mystery inspire you to seek
the power behind this magnificent creation.

DAY 283

Honor your questions; seek your answers.

DAY 284

If you don't take charge of your mind's activity, your life may be dominated by worry, rumination, or trivial commentary that distracts you from your purpose. It's as if your radio is tuned between stations, and you just listen to the static rather than changing the station. The solution is to tune in to a meaningful channel, where the wisdom of your true self—not the chatter of the ego—is the voice you hear in your mind.

DAY 285

No matter where the focus of our discomfort
lies, we can change our lives by taking charge of
our perceptions and attitudes. We can let go of
thoughts that life should be different, replacing
these judgments with acceptance and gratitude.

DAY 286

When you find yourself worrying or ruminating,
choose instead to practice inquiry. Start by
investigating the day-to-day needs of the
self: "Why am I in this state? How can I get
better?" Then expand the range of inquiry
until you are covering life's biggest questions.

DAY 287

Spiritual inquiry – not worry – is the best
utilization of your brainpower. Worry
drains your energy without creating any real
change. Inquiry expands your consciousness,
bringing you wisdom and understanding.

DAY 288

In inquiry, we dance between mystery and what's
known. We are captivated by the desire to learn.

DAY 289

Inquiry offers us a way to overcome
mental chaos. Anxiety, depression,
worry, and stress fall away.

DAY 290

Divine presence does not need to be proven;
it needs to be perceived by the wondering
minds and hearts of those who seek.

DAY 291

When you focus on life's biggest questions,
you become able to detach yourself from
the little things and move your attention
to consciously creating a life based on
your purpose, dreams, and desires.

DAY 292

As children, we have no notion past, present
and future; we are always present. When we
grow up, life demands that we make things
happen, so our consciousness shifts. But when
we hold too tightly to notions of past and future,
we destroy our own peace of mind. We can be
ourselves and express ourselves only when we
are consciously present. We are meant to learn
when to use our awareness of past and future
and when to let go and be in the here and now.

Purpose

DAY 293

The moment we realize that there's meaning
to our existence, we hear the unmistakable
calling of the soul's desires. We naturally start to
embrace a sense of responsibility and purpose.

DAY 294

We are meant to resolve the greatest of
human inquiries: to find the answers
to our most persistent and pressing
questions about the meaning of life.

DAY 295

The Divine has placed you on earth for a reason.

DAY 296

Purpose will always be something bigger
than yourself. It will always pull you toward
its center to experience the true relief of
suffering. Your job is to surrender to its pull.

DAY 297

If your heart can see clearly that this life
was created by a Divine being, then your
heart will tell you that there is a divine
purpose for your life. With your conscious
participation, your life story will unfold in a
way that reveals and fulfills that purpose.

DAY 298

When we witness the chaotic, violent, and unpredictable events taking place around the world, it's natural to be deeply troubled. We may wish to be of service but not know what to do or where to begin. How can we possibly make any difference? Each of us has a vital role to play in restoring peace and harmony to the world. To fulfill the intention of your creation, you must discover your unique role.

DAY 299

We live in challenging times, with accelerating change and widespread upheaval. Each of us is called upon to contemplate how our unique gifts can be applied not just in our immediate circles, but more broadly.

DAY 300

Rather than simply reacting to the
pleasant or unpleasant distractions that
are presented to us, we must choose to act
from what is within us. This is living from
the inside out, not from the outside in.

DAY 301

We are called on to return to our hearts,
return to God, and embrace the precious gift
of existence. To take our true place in the
universe, we must seek God in all that we do.

DAY 302

In listening to our hearts, we set aside the
external rules and regain our own power.
We follow that which is right and that which
is of the highest truth and integrity.

DAY 303

Times of change and unpredictability
can lead you to your life purpose.

DAY 304

By cultivating our connection to the
Divine, we find not just a generic meaning
of life but the meaning of our own life.

DAY 305

Every soul comes with a figurative fingerprint,
a blend of God-given gifts and talents. The
soul seeks ways to bring forth its uniqueness.
What does your soul long to express?

DAY 306

As a child, what did you most love to do? How
did you choose to spend your free time? What
were your favorite realms of imagination?
What were your childhood dreams? What did
you most want to become or accomplish? These
are the early manifestations of your gifts, and
they can be geared toward a higher purpose.

DAY 307

Ways of expressing your soul's uniqueness
can vary, from speaking your truth about
a certain situation to finding the courage
to stand up for yourself to making art
that brings beauty to the world.

DAY 308

You become stronger from the inside
as you know who you really are and
what you want to do in this world.

DAY 309

We can find true peace and happiness
only when we know what it is that we
are meant to do with our lives.

DAY 310

When we recognize our unique gifts, we express
the purpose imprinted within us by the Divine.

DAY 311

A life lived with purpose is the most precious
gift you can give to yourself and to the
world. That's how you become part of the
solution and help restore peace, harmony,
and the magnificence of the human race.

DAY 312

When talent meets service, your passion
becomes your life purpose. You bring
authenticity to the world. You live with fluidity,
joy, and an entirely new level of well-being.

DAY 313

Life becomes effortless when you
understand how the universe operates
and what you are here to do.

Prayer

DAY 314

At any time, no matter what's happening, you
can use prayer to move yourself forward.

DAY 315

To pray for yourself is a form of self-love.

DAY 316

Prayer isn't just about asking for what you want
in the first place. It's an ongoing practice of
communication with the Divine. You can use it
to express gratitude for the goodness in your life.
You can use it to help yourself through a difficult
situation. During periods of waiting, prayer
can help you keep your vision and goals alive.

DAY 317

Alignment with the Divine is the delicate combined state of surrender and prayer. In alignment, you move and act the same way the rest of God's creations do, secure in your awareness of the higher power that guides you. At the same time, you are in a constant state of prayer, of personal communication with the Divine, to ask for what you need and express your gratitude and praise.

DAY 318

Surrender is the art of operating in a governed universe by cultivating an intimate relationship with the Divine. You step into a sacred circle that rotates with input both from you and from the Divine. In that circle, prayer is your input. At the same time, you allow guidance and input from the Divine by wholeheartedly surrendering your actions and listening in. In this way, the Divine shapes your life with wisdom and grace.

DAY 319

Many of us think that prayer is asking for what
we want, but it goes far beyond that. Prayer is
the breathing in and out of the universal truths.

DAY 320

We nourish ourselves spiritually when we
cultivate the daily practices that support us
in hearing and voicing the truth of all there
is. We expand into the natural state of joy.

DAY 321

Religion can ground your spirituality
in consistent practice.

DAY 322

Prayer is the song of a dedicated heart.

DAY 323

When you pray, God listens.

DAY 324

A prayer has the power to change your destiny.

DAY 325

Prayer can be a call for divine intervention.
It is a declaration that we have reached
the limits of our sphere of influence.

DAY 326

Prayer goes beyond asking for what you need.
Your actions can also be your prayers. As you
act in prayer, your soul expresses its uniqueness
and its qualities of goodness. Good works
come from your open and giving heart. There's
no one specific thing you are doing to change
the world. You are giving to the world, not by
forcing yourself to contribute but by heeding
your soul's eager call to express its gifts.

DAY 327

In prayer, the soul gets to express its beauty
and essence through acts of kindness. It
gets to show the world its unique signature,
and it brings life to the lives of others.

DAY 328

The most authentic and genuine form
of gratitude is the one that comes from
a heart that has truly recognized the
Divine gifts given to us every day. When
you are content, you are grateful.

DAY 329

When things aren't unfolding as you expect,
you can use prayer to clarify your intentions
and align them with the needs of your soul.

DAY 330

An open and intimate relationship with the
Divine is available to you without any sort
of medium or middleman. You have direct
access to the Divine at any moment.

Surrender

DAY 331

What does it mean to surrender? It is a
declaration of your heart that you give
yourself—your life, your path, your destiny,
and your soul—over to your Creator.

DAY 332

When you find and know the Divine, your
heart can't help but surrender to the larger
prayer that has been whispered by the rest
of creation since the beginning of time.

DAY 333

Whatever you wish to accomplish, the practice of surrendering to the Divine will move you forward with grace.

DAY 334

True enlightenment happens when the self sheds its ego to see the light of God.

DAY 335

Paradoxically, surrender is the most powerful action we can take.

DAY 336

The journey to find and connect with
Source naturally culminates in surrender
to the Divine. The moment of surrender is a
moment of deep openness of the soul. It is
an invitation to trust the Divine while you
open your heart to the unknown. The soul
sighs as it finally recognizes that Source is
available to support it through its journey.

DAY 337

In times of uncertainty, nothing is guaranteed,
and that's why we must enter the sacred
circle of surrender and prayer. That is
exactly what we need in order to thrive.

DAY 338

When life is uncertain, there's no door
open but the one of surrender.

DAY 339

Surrender is not a temporary practice, and
it is not to be practiced only during times of
crisis and then abandoned once the crisis is
over. Surrender is an integral element in a
life that is well lived. It is a constant state
of being that the soul seeks to achieve.

DAY 340

Surrender is something you practice both
with your heart and with your mind.

DAY 341

When you begin to live a life of surrender to
the Divine, you will notice that your well-being
dramatically improves. You will also notice
that your worries and stresses start to lift.
Your soul will expand in the presence of the
truth as you steer your life toward the Light.

DAY 342

Your soul recognizes its oneness with the rest of
creation, and it knows where it has come from.
The soul surrenders easily to unity of Source.

DAY 343

Finding and connecting to the Divine
frees us from struggle and fear by
teaching us to surrender that which is
beyond our influence. While it may be
unsettling to think that we cannot always
determine the outcomes, surrender has
infinite power to soothe our anxiety.

DAY 344

What a relief to know that it is not all up to
us! Life is a journey in which we are guided
and supported every step of the way.

DAY 345

Whatever changes you desire in your life, true success depends not only on your own effort but also on surrendering to the Divine. It is surrender that allows us to go far beyond ordinary goals to fulfill our true purpose in life.

DAY 346

Surrendering is about making room for change in your life while allowing the Divine plan to unfold. You make plans and set intentions, but at the same time you allow the "how" to emerge into your experience.

DAY 347

It's possible to become caught up in the effort of
trying to make things work, not knowing that
we can achieve the same outcomes perfectly and
harmoniously when we surrender and pray.

DAY 348

When you commit to purposeful living, you
give your life and your path over to your
Creator; you wholeheartedly say, "Guide me.
Take care of me. I am here to acknowledge the
truth about you while I do good in the world."

DAY 349

Surrender is far more than a remedy or
coping mechanism. It is a way of life. In fact,
given the limits of our power and control,
surrender is always our only real option.

DAY 350

Surrender requires you to understand
both your responsibility and the
limits of your responsibility.

DAY 351

There's an element of unpredictability in everything we do. In the space of unpredictability, we have a choice between trying hard and letting go.

DAY 352

There's a subtle difference between surrender and letting go. In surrender, you take action to move things forward, and then you shift into waiting. While you wait, you feed the energy of your desire through prayer, positive thinking, visualization, and planning. The energy of the desire is alive in your heart even while you wait. If you let go in the sense of giving up, the energy of the desire fades away, and the dream becomes unattainable.

DAY 353

We can choose to surrender, just like fish swimming downstream not knowing where they will end up. All they know is that it is time to migrate and move. They understand it to be part of their purpose in life; they just can't see into the future, so they rely on the Divine to guide them on their way downstream. They trust and surrender, knowing that life moves on effortlessly and graciously. A new life will be waiting for them when they arrive.

DAY 354

Surrender is about knowing when to "do"—when to exert our influence—and when to simply "be."

DAY 355

Surrender is not easy, but it is much
easier to surrender than to try to hold
everything together by ourselves.

DAY 356

Where our individual powers end, the Divine
is waiting for us. We arrive at the limits of
what we can do on our own, and so we knock
on the door of the Divine. When we do that,
the Divine responds with love and grace.

DAY 357

On the path of surrender, we use our free will to do good in the world while releasing our grasp on the outcome.

DAY 358

Surrendering does not mean you do not make choices. Nor does it mean that you do nothing. Surrender in and of itself is a choice we consciously make when we realize that we need Divine guidance.

DAY 359

Surrendering cannot be done halfway. It
requires our wholehearted commitment.

DAY 360

Surrender need not be a struggle. It is
the state your soul longs to be in, the
home place it knows how to navigate.

DAY 361

When you enter with the Divine into the
sacred circle of prayer and surrender, you yield
control and receive love and protection.

DAY 362

No one else has any power over you. People and situations are merely mirrors and guides on your journey. There's no power that resides outside of you except the power of the Divine.

DAY 363

When you wholeheartedly practice surrender, every aspect of your life becomes a prayer. You understand the purpose of your creation, and you embody it in your actions. You create a life that fulfills the soul's need to find and connect to its Divine creator, to be in its unique states, and to express itself fully.

DAY 364

The door is wide open to each and every
one of us. The way of the Light is there
for those who understand the profound
connection between humans and nature, for
those who see the inseparable bond calling
to be acknowledged and recognized.

Day 365

At the end of our journey, we can't help but surrender. We can't help but sing our love and praise for the creative power that brought us here as we bow in awe to the gift of existence.

Also Available by the author

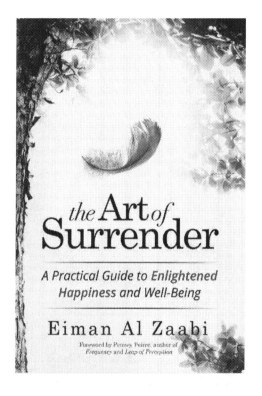

The Art of Surrender: A Practical Guide to
Enlightened Happiness and Well-being